Baritone/Bass Volume 1
Revised Edition

W9-CED-730

THE
SINGERS
MUSICAL THEATRE
ANTHOLOGY

A collection of songs from the musical stage, categorized by voice type. The selections are presented in their authentic settings, excerpted from the original vocal scores.

ISBN 0-88188-548-7

HAL•LEONARD®
CORPORATION
7777 W. BLUEMOUND RD. P.O. BOX 13819 MILWAUKEE, WI 53213

Visit Hal Leonard Online at
www.halleonard.com

Foreword

The Singer's Musical Theatre Anthology is the most comprehensive series of its kind ever to appear in print. Its unique perspective is in looking at the field of musical theatre in terms of vocal literature. One of the prime parameters in choosing the songs for this series was that they should all be, in some way, particularly vocally gratifying.

Many of the songs included here are very familiar to us, yet we seldom see them printed as they were originally written and performed. The long tradition in sheet music throughout this century has been to adapt a song in several ways to conform to a format which makes it accessible to the average pianist. This type of arrangement is what one finds in vocal selections, or in any piano/vocal collection of show music. These sheet arrangements serve their purpose very well, but aren't really the best performing editions for a singer. In contrast, the selections in this series have been excerpted from the original vocal scores. One of the many benefits of this is a much more satisfying piano accompaniment. In addition, many songs here have never been available separately from the full vocal scores.

In some cases, a song has required some adaptation in order to be excerpted from a show's vocal score. The practice of performing arias as removed from their operatic context gives many precedents for making such adjustments. In many ways, one could view this anthology as a "performing edition." Significant editorial adjustments are indicated by footnotes in some instances.

The original keys of this literature (which are used here) can give important information to a singer about the nature of a song and how it should sound, and in most cases they will work very well for most singers. But, unlike opera, these original keys do not necessarily need to be reverently maintained. With some musical theatre literature, a singer should not rule out transposing a song up or down for vocal comfort.

There is certainly no codified system for classifying theatre music as to voice type. With some roles the classification is obvious. With others there is a good deal of ambiguity. As a result, a particular singer might find suitable literature in this anthology in both volumes of his/her gender.

Any performer of these songs will benefit greatly by a careful study of the show and role from which any given song is taken. This type of approach is taken for granted with an actor preparing a monologue or an opera singer preparing an aria. But because much theatre music has been the popular music of its time, we sometimes easily lose awareness of its dramatic context.

The selections in **The Singer's Musical Theatre Anthology** will certainly be significant additions to a singer's repertory, but no anthology can include every wonderful song. There is a vast body of literature, some of it virtually unknown, waiting to be discovered and brought to life.

The Revised Edition adds eight musically diverse and attractive selections, making the volume more useful to more singers. The additions are: "I Am the Very Model," "Marian the Librarian," "Marry Me a Little," "Reviewing the Situation," "River in the Rain," "Ten Minutes Ago," "When I Was a Lad" and "When You're Lying Awake." The *Sweeney Todd* song "Johanna," though very suitable to lyric baritones in its original key, has been moved to the Tenor volume at the request of tenors and teachers.

Richard Walters, editor

THE SINGER'S MUSICAL THEATRE ANTHOLOGY

Baritone/Bass

Contents

ABOUT THE SHOWS

*The material in this section is by Stanley Green, Richard Walters, and Robert Viagas,
some of which was previously published elsewhere.*

ANYONE CAN WHISTLE

MUSIC AND LYRICS: Stephen Sondheim
BOOK: Arthur Laurents
DIRECTOR: Arthur Laurents
CHOREOGRAPHER: Herbert Ross
OPENED: 4/4/64, New York

Something of a "cult" musical, *Anyone Can Whistle* is an allegorical satire in which Angela Lansbury (in her first Broadway musical) played a corrupt mayor of a bankrupt town who comes up with a scheme to attract tourists: a fake miracle in which a stream of water appears to spout out of a solid rock. The town soon becomes a mecca for the gullible and the pious, but the hoax is exposed when the inmates of a mental institution called the Cookie Jar get mixed up with the pilgrims. Harry Guardino played a candidate for the booby hatch mistaken for the new doctor, and Lee Remick was the head nurse, so inhibited, she was unable to whistle.

BIG RIVER

MUSIC AND LYRICS: Roger Miller
BOOK: William Hauptman
DIRECTOR: Des McAnuff
CHOREOGRAPHER: Janet Watson
OPENED: 4/25/85, New York

The show is based on Mark Twain's American classic, *The Adventures of Huckleberry Finn*, about an early 19th century Missouri boy who tries to help a runaway slave escape to the North, but accidentally winds up riding with him on a raft down the Mississippi into the deep South. Along the way they explore a country full of fraud and hate, but also full of innocence and even beauty. The Tony-winning show featured a score from country songwriter Roger Miller ("King of the Road"). As the title suggests, *Big River* (including even the set) evoked the river as constantly present, almost as character in the play. And in a reflective moment, Huck gazes out over the stormswept water and sings "River in the Rain," wondering where it will carry him next.

CAMELOT

MUSIC: Frederick Loewe
LYRICS AND BOOK: Alan Jay Lerner
DIRECTOR: Moss Hart
CHOREOGRAPHER: Hanya Holm
OPENED: 12/3/60, New York

Lerner and Loewe's first Broadway production following their spectacular hit *My Fair Lady*, was another musical based on a highly esteemed work of British fiction, T.H. White's novel, *The Once and Future King*. Again, too, they were joined by fair lady Julie Andrews and director Moss Hart for an opulently mounted retelling of the Arthurian legend, with its high-minded knights of the round table and its tragic romantic triangle involving King Arthur, his queen Guenevere, and his trusted knight, Sir Lancelot. Helped by a huge advance ticket sale, *Camelot* easily surmounted a divided press to become something of a Broadway legend itself—providing imagery (eventually all too apt) for the administration of President John F. Kennedy who used to play the cast album in the White House. In 1980, during a tour headed by Richard Burton (the original King Arthur), *Camelot* returned to New York to play the New York State Theatre for 56 performances. After Burton was succeeded on the road by Richard Harris, the musical came back again, this time to the Winter Garden for an additional 48 performances. In 1967 Joshua Logan directed Mr. Harris opposite Vanessa Redgrave in the Warner Bros. film version.

CAROUSEL

MUSIC: Richard Rodgers
LYRICS AND BOOK: Oscar Hammerstein II
CHOREOGRAPHER: Agnes de Mille
DIRECTOR: Rouben Mamoulian
OPENED: 4/19/45, New York

The collaborators of *Oklahoma!* chose Ferenc Molnar's *Liliom* as the basis for their second show. Oscar Hammerstein shifted Molnar's Budapest locale to a late nineteenth century fishing village in New England. The two principal roles are Billy Bigelow, a shiftless carnival barker, and Julie Jordan, an ordinary factory worker. This is not merely a simple boy meets girl plot, but contains a predominant theme of tragedy throughout most of the play. The score is rich with musical high points, the first coming with "If I Loved You," sung by Julie and Billy at their first meeting. Billy's famous "Soliloquy" is Richard Rodgers longest and most operatic song, and can truly be considered an aria. The show was presented in a major Broadway revival (a production which originated in London) in 1994.

CINDERELLA

MUSIC: Richard Rodgers
LYRICS AND BOOK: Oscar Hammerstein II
DIRECTOR: Ralph Nelson
CHOREOGRAPHER: Jonathan Lucas
FIRST AIRED: 3/31/57 on CBS-TV

Ever the innovators, Rodgers and Hammerstein were among the first to explore the new medium of television with a full-length original TV musical. The original broadcast also was fortunate in securing the services of Julie Andrews, fresh from her triumph as the Cinderella-like heroine of *My Fair Lady*. In adapting the children's fairy tale, Hammerstein was careful not to alter or update the familiar story about a young woman who collaborates with her Fairy Godmother to overcome the plots of her evil stepmother and stepsisters so she can go to an opulent ball and meet a handsome prince. Cinderella still loses her magical glass slipper, and the Prince proclaims that he will marry the girl whose foot fits the slipper. Because the original production was filmed live and could not be preserved except in black-and-white kinescope, a new production was captured on tape in 1965. Starring Lesley Ann Warren, this second version is the one that's been aired numerous times and even released on video. A stage adaptation toured the U.S., and the musical finally made its New York stage debut in 1993 at New York City Opera, with Christa Moore as Cinderella. At the ball, the prince is stunned by how quickly he's fallen in love with this ravishing stranger, and sings the waltzing "Ten Minutes Ago" (a duet with Cinderella in the original). An opulent new version was made for television in 1998, with pop singer Brandy in the title role and Bernadette Peters as the stepmother.

COMPANY

MUSIC AND LYRICS: Stephen Sondheim
BOOK: George Furth
DIRECTOR: Harold Prince
CHOREOGRAPHER: Michael Bennett
OPENED: 4/26/70, New York

Company was the first of the Sondheim musicals to have been directed by Harold Prince, and more than any other musical, reflects America in the 1970s. The show is a plotless evening about five affluent couples living in a Manhattan apartment building, and their excessively protective feelings about a charming, but somewhat indifferent bachelor named Bobby. They want to fix him up and see him married, even though it's clear their own marriages are far from perfect. In the end he seems ready to take the plunge. The songs are often very sophisticated, expressing the ambivalent or caustic attitudes of fashionable New Yorkers of the time. Making a connection with another person, the show seems to say, is the key to happiness. Bobby's fear of commitment is obvious in "Marry Me a Little," in which he pleads for a relationship that goes only so deep and no deeper. The number was cut from the original production but restored as an Act I finale in the 1995 Broadway revival. An Off-Broadway revue of Sondheim songs also borrowed the song title as its overall title. "Sorry-Grateful" expresses the often ambivalent or caustic attitudes of sophisticated New Yorkers.

THE FANTASTICKS

MUSIC: Harvey Schimdt
LYRICS AND BOOK: Tom Jones
DIRECTOR: Word Baker
OPENED: 5/3/60, New York

The statistics alone are, well, fantastic. Since *The Fantasticks* opened over 40 years ago at a tiny Greenwich Village theatre, there have been, to date, many thousands of productions in the United States, fifteen touring companies, hundreds of productions in more than 66 foreign countries, and the backers have received more than 10,000% profit on their initial investment of $16,500. No other production, on or off Broadway, has ever enjoyed such a lengthy run. Curiously, the initial reviews were either mixed or negative, and producer Lore Noto seriously considered closing the show after its first discouraging week. But an Off-Broadway award, the popularity of the song "Try to Remember," and, most important, word of mouth, all helped to turn the show's fortunes around.

The fragile fantasy is concerned with the theme of seasonal rebirth, or the paradox of "why Spring is born out of Winter's laboring pain." In the story, adapted from Edmond Rostand's play, *Les Ramanesques*, the fathers of two youthful lovers, Luisa and Matt, feel they must show parental disapproval to make sure that their progenies remain together. When this deception is revealed, the lovers quarrel and Matt goes off to seek adventure. At the end, after a number of degrading experiences, he returns to Luisa's waiting arms.

FOLLIES

MUSIC AND LYRICS: Stephen Sondheim
BOOK: James Goldman
DIRECTOR: Harold Prince
CHOREOGRAPHER: Michael Bennett
OPENED: 4/4/71, New York

Taking place at a reunion of former *Ziegfeld Follies*-type showgirls, the musical deals with the reality of life as contrasted with the unreality of the theatre. *Follies* explores this theme through the lives of two couples, the upper-class, unhappy, Phyllis and Benjamin Stone, and the middle-class, also unhappy, Sally and Buddy Plummer. *Follies* also shows us these four as they were in their pre-marital youth. The young actors appear as ghosts to haunt their elder selves. Because the show is about the past, and often in flashback, Sondheim styled his songs to evoke some of the theatre's great composers and lyricists of the past, with a cast that suggests some of the vivid personalities of 1920s Broadway. The show was given two concert performances in September of 1985 at Avery Fisher Hall in New York City, with a cast that included Barbara Cook, George Hearn, Mandy Patinkin, Lee Remick, Carol Burnett and many others. A new recording of the musical was released as a result of these performances. A very complete new recording of the show, with all cut numbers, was released in 1996. At this writing, a Broadway revival is scheduled for 2001.

HMS PINAFORE

MUSIC: Arthur Sullivan
LIBRETTO: W.S. Gilbert
OPENED: May 25, 1878, the Opera Comique, London

The beauty of satire is that it can mock both sides of an issue. Here the twin targets are the inviolable British class structure and the accompanying naive pretensions of egalitarianism. The curtain rises on Her Majesty's ship *Pinafore*, newly docked in Portsmouth and preparing for inspection by Sir Joseph Porter, First Lord of the Admiralty. When Sir Joseph arrives on board, he tells of his rise from office boy to "the ruler of the Queen's Navee" ("When I Was a Lad"). Captain Corcoran, commander of the *Pinafore*, has arranged for his daughter Josephine to wed Sir Joseph, though she is secretly in love with Ralph Rackstraw, a common sailor. Sir Joseph talks a good game about equality, but in the end—after numerous turns of plot and the obligatory cases of mistaken identity—he, along with everyone else, is constrained, even comforted, by the boundaries of class.

IOLANTHE

MUSIC: Arthur Sullivan
LIBRETTO: W.S. Gilbert
OPENED: November 25, 1882, the Savoy Theatre, London

Iolanthe, a fairy, had committed the capital offense of marrying a mortal, but was granted exile rather than death. After twenty-five years, the fairy Queen allows her to rejoin elfin society. Meanwhile, Iolanthe's son Strephon, who is half fairy (from the waist up) has fallen in love with young Phyllis, ward of the Lord Chancellor. But the latter will not consent to their marriage. In fact, he's been trying, unsuccessfully, to petition himself for her hand, and the turmoil is giving him nightmares ("When You're Lying Awake"). In the end, Iolanthe clears the way for Strephon and Phyllis to be wed by appealing to the Lord Chancellor, who turns out to be her husband, and who had believed her to be dead. When the entire fairy court reveals that they have married the House of Lords, the fairy Queen is in a quandary: she can't sentence them all to death. Fortunately, the Lord Chancellor, experienced in these matters, changes fairy law with a quick bit of legislative chicanery, the Lords all sprout wings, and everyone flies off happily to Fairyland.

MUSIC AND LYRICS: Cole Porter
BOOK: Samuel and Bella Spewack
DIRECTOR: John C. Wilson
CHOREOGRAPHER: Hanya Holm
OPENED: 12/30/48, New York

The genesis of Cole Porter's longest-running musical occurred in 1935 when producer Saint Subber, then a stagehand for the Theatre Guild's production of Shakespeare's *Taming of the Shrew*, became aware that its stars Alfred Lunt and Lynn Fontanne, quarreled almost as much in private as did the characters in the play. Years later he offered this parallel story as the basis for a musical comedy to the same writing trio, Porter and the Spewacks, who had already worked on the successful show, *Leave It To Me!* The entire action of *Kiss Me, Kate* occurs backstage and onstage at Ford's Theatre, Baltimore, during a tryout of a musical version of *The Taming of the Shrew*. The main plot concerns the egotisitical actor-producer Fred Graham and his temperamental ex-wife Lili Vanessi who—like Shakespeare's Petruchio and Kate—fight and make up and eventually demonstrate their enduring affection for each other. One of the chief features of the score is the skillful way Cole Porter combined his own musical world ("So In Love," "Too Darn Hot," and "Why Can't You Behabe?") with Shakespeare's world ("I Hate Men"), while also tossing off a Viennese waltz parody ("Wunderbar") and a comic view of the Bard's plays ("Brush Up Your Shakespeare"). MGM's 1953 screen version, under George Sidney's direction, had a cast headed by Howard Keel, Kathryn Grayson, and Ann Miller. The 1999 Broadway revival was highly acclaimed, plugging new life to the classic show.

KNICKERBOCKER HOLIDAY

MUSIC: Kurt Weill
LYRICS AND BOOK: Maxwell Anderson
DIRECTOR: Joshua Logan
OPENED: 10/19/38, New York

In spite of its relatively short run, *Knickerbocker Holiday* is considered a significant milestone on Broadway. In one of the first musicals to use a historical subject to comment on contemporary political problems, its anti-fascist theme pitted democracy against totalitarianism in retelling the reign of Governor Stuyvesant in New Amsterdam in 1647. The story tells how the governor intervenes on behalf of an independent and troublesome knife sharpener, Brom Broeck, who has been arbitrarily selected by the council to be executed on a trumped up charge, mainly because they had no one to hang. When the father of Tina (Brom's true love) offers his daughter's hand in marriage to the governor, Stuyvesant reveals his feeling about love and growing old in the touching "September Song." The reactionary governor proceeds to abolish whatever freedoms the town had previously enjoyed, and when Brom protests, throws him in jail. But Brom, the freedom loving "first American" escapes and steals the Governor's intended bride. The musical was one of the earliest of Kurt Weill's shows written in America, after his own flight from the totalitarianism of Nazi Germany.

LOST IN THE STARS

MUSIC: Kurt Weill
LYRICS AND BOOK: Maxwell Anderson
DIRECTOR: Rouben Mamoulian
OPENED: 10/30/49, New York

Kurt Weill's final Broadway musical (his second in collaboration with Maxwell Anderson) was written to convey "a message of hope that people, through a personal approach, will solve whatever racial problems that exist." In the idealistic story, adapted from Alan Paton's *Cry, the Beloved Country*, the action is set in and around Johannesburg, South Africa. Absalom Kumalo, the errant son of a black minister, Stephen Kumalo, accidentally kills a white man in a robbery attempt and is condemned to hang. The tragedy, however, leads to a sympathetic bond between Stephen and James Jarvis, the dead man's father, which gives some indication that understanding between the races can be achieved in the land of apartheid. A newer version, presented by Ely Landau's American Film theatre, was shown in 1974 with a cast headed by Brock Peters and Melba Moore.

LOVE LIFE

MUSIC: Kurt Weill
LYRICS AND BOOK: Alan Jay Lerner
DIRECTOR: Elia Kazan
CHOREOGRAPHER: Michael Kidd
OPENED: 10/7/48, New York

On hiatus from his partnership with composer Frederick Loewe, Alan Jay Lerner collaborated with Kurt Weill on this musical allegory. *Love Life*, termed by its authors as simply "a vaudeville," chronicled the fluctuations of the archetypal Sam and Susan Cooper's marriage through 157 years of American history from 1791 to 1948. The story shows how the growing tensions of modern life make it increasingly difficult for the couple to maintain their matrimonial equilibrium. This ambitious, surreal story is told through ragtime, blues, a madrigal, a ballet, clog dancing, ventriloquism, a minstrel show, and even tightrope walking. Fans have regarded the show as structurally innovative and ahead of its time.

MAN OF LA MANCHA

MUSIC: Mitch Leigh
LYRICS: Joe Darlon
BOOK: Dale Wasserman
CHOREOGRAPHER: Jack Cole
DIRECTOR: Albert Marre
OPENED: 11/22/65, New York

Cervantes' great demented hero, Don Quixote, is the unlikely hero of this very popular musical of the '60s. Although very much rooted in the Spanish novelist's work, this musical version was adapted from Dale Wasserman's television play, *I, Don Quixote*. The principal characters, besides Don Quixote, are Sancho Panza, the Don's squire and sidekick, and Aldonza, who Quixote sees as his grand lady, Dulcinea. Richard Kiley was the original New York Don, certainly one of the best baritone roles in musical theatre literature. The film version, released in 1972, starred Peter O'Toole and Sophia Loren.

THE MUSIC MAN

MUSIC, LYRICS AND BOOK: Meredith Willson
DIRECTOR: Morton Da Costa
CHOREOGRAPHER: Onna White
OPENED: 12/19/57, New York

With *The Music Man*, composer-lyricist-librettist Meredith Willson recaptured the innocent charm of the middle American Iowa town where he grew up. It is the Fourth of July, 1912, and the abundantly charming "Professor" Harold Hill, actually a traveling con man, arrives in River City, Iowa ready to work his latest scam. He poses as a professor of music, collecting money for lessons and instruments on the promise that he can teach the town's children how to play in a marching band through his fraudulent "Think System." But his plans to pocket the cash and skip town are complicated by the presence of the temptingly pretty Marian Paroo, the librarian and music teacher. She sees through him immediately, but is soon won over by the palpable excitement he's able to generate among the stuffy townspeople—and in her formerly withdrawn younger brother. The story ends with a touch of theatre magic. Just as the townspeople are about to tar and feather Hill, lo and behold, the Think System works, and the kids are able to play! The show, which took eight years and more than thirty rewrites before it was produced on Broadway, marked Willson's auspicious debut in the theatre. It was also the first musical-stage appearance by Robert Preston, playing the role of Harold Hill, who went on to repeat his dynamic performance in the 1962 Warner Bros. screen version. A 1980 Broadway revival starred Dick Van Dyke, and Broadway had another visit from the professor in spring 2000. A sly, predatory rhythm underpins "Marian the Librarian," Hill's song of courtship as he stalks her among the shelves of her library.

OKLAHOMA!

MUSIC: Richard Rodgers
LYRICS AND BOOK: Oscar Hammerstein II
CHOREOGRAPHER: Agnes de Mille
DIRECTOR: Rouben Mamoulian
OPENED: 3/31/43, New York

There are many reasons why *Oklahoma!* is a recognized landmark in the history of the American musical theatre. In the initial collaboration between Richard Rodgers and Oscar Hammerstein II, it not only expertly fused the major elements in the production—story, songs and dances—it also utilized dream ballets to reveal hidden desires and fears of the principals. In addition, the musical, based on Lynn Riggs' play, *Green Grow the Lilacs*, was the first with a book that honestly depicted the kind of rugged pioneers who had once tilled the land and tended the cattle. Set in Indian Territory soon after the turn of the century, *Oklahoma!* spins a simple tale mostly concerned with whether the decent Curly or the menacing Jud gets to take Laurey to the box social. Though she chooses Jud in a fit of pique, Laurey really loves Curly and they soon make plans to marry. At their wedding they join in celebrating Oklahoma's impending statehood, then—after Jud is accidentally killed in a fight with Curly—the couple ride off in their surrey with the fringe on top. With its Broadway run of five years, nine months, *Oklahoma!* established a long-run record that it held for fifteen years. It also toured the United States and Canada for over a decade. In 1979, the musical was revived on Broadway with a cast headed by Laurence Guittard and Christine Andreas, and ran for 293 performances. The film version, the first in Todd-AO, was released by Magna in 1955. Gordon MacRae, Shirley Jones and Charlotte Greenwood were in it, and the director was Fred Zinnemann.

OLIVER!

MUSIC, LYRICS AND BOOK: Lionel Bart
DIRECTOR: Peter Coe
OPENED: 6/30/60, London
　　　　　　1/6/63, New York

Oliver! established Lionel Bart as Britain's outstanding musical theatre talent of the 1960s, at a time when the form was almost completely dominated by Americans. Until overtaken by *Jesus Christ Superstar* in the 1970s, *Oliver!* held the record as the longest–running musical in British history. Based on Charles Dickens' novel, the musical follows the orphan Oliver Twist and his adventures as a member of a pickpocket crew in the underworld of Victorian London, working for a wily old master thief named Fagin. *Oliver!* also had the longest run of any British musical presented in New York in the 1960s. The show was revived on Broadway in 1984. In 1968 it was made into an Academy Award-winning movie produced by Columbia. In the comic "Reviewing the Situation," Fagin tries to imagine the pleasures of the honest life—but upon closer examination they just don't seem to hold up.

PAINT YOUR WAGON

MUSIC: Frederick Loewe
LYRICS AND BOOK: Alan Jay Lerner
CHOREOGRAPHER: Agnes de Mille
DIRECTOR: Daniel Mann
OPENED: 11/12/51, New York

Filling their musical play with authentic incidents and backgrounds, Lerner and Loewe struck it rich both musically and dramatically with a work that captured all the flavor of the roistering, robust California gold prospectors of 1853. James Barton, returning to the musical stage for the first time in twenty years, took the part of Ben Rumson, a grizzled prospector whose daughter Jennifer (Olga San Juan) discovers gold near their camp. Word of the strike quickly spreads and before long there are over 4,000 inhabitants in the new town of Rumson. Jennifer, who has fallen in love with Julio, a Mexican (Tony Bavaar), goes East to school but returns to Julio when the gold strike peters out, Rumson is virtually a ghost town, and Ben is left with nothing but his hopes and dreams. Paramount's 1969 screen version used a different story. In the leading roles were Clint Eastwood, Lee Marvin, and Jean Seberg, and Joshua Logan was the director.

THE PIRATES OF PENZANCE

MUSIC: Arthur Sullivan
LIBRETTO: W.S. Gilbert
OPENED: December 31, 1879, New York

The only one of Gilbert and Sullivan's works to have its official premiere outside London, it did in fact receive one prior performance in England for purposes of copyright registration. Twenty-one-year-old Frederic, bound by his sense of duty to serve out his apprenticeship to a band of pirates, has reached the end of his indentures and decides henceforth to oppose the cutthroat crew rather than join them. After leaving the pirates, Frederic happens upon a party of young women and appeals to them for pity. The pirates then arrive on the scene, determined to marry the young ladies, but the girls' father, Major-General Stanley, enters just in time and wins clemency by claiming to be an orphan. Frederic, at first duty-bound to destroy his former comrades, rejoins them when he find that his apprenticeship extends to his twenty-first birthday, and, having been born on February 29, he has so far had only five birthdays. But in the end, the pirates yield to the police at the invocation of Queen Victoria's name, and when it is revealed that they are actually wayward noblemen, they earn their pardon and permission to marry the Major-General's daughters.

PORGY AND BESS

MUSIC: George Gershwin
LYRICS: Ira Gershwin and DuBose Heyward
LIBRETTO: DuBose Heyward
DIRECTOR: Rouben Mamoulian
OPENED: 10/10/35, New York

Universally recognized as the most esteemed and popular opera written by an American composer, *Porgy and Bess* began in 1925 as a novel called *Porgy* by DuBose Heyward. Heyward's setting of Catfish Row in Charleston, South Carolina, and his emotional story of the cripple beggar Porgy, the seductive Bess, the menacing Crown, and the slinky cocaine dealer Sportin' Life, fired Gershwin's imagination even before Heyward and his wife, Dorothy, transformed the book into a play two years later. After many delays, Gershwin, with Heyward and the composer's brother Ira, began writing the opera late in 1933, and completed it—including orchestrations—in twenty months. The initial Broadway production, with Todd Duncan and Anne Brown in the title roles, was not a commercial success, though many of the solos and duets—"Summertime," "Bess, You Is My Woman Now," "I Got Plenty O' Nuttin'," "It Ain't Necessarily So" for example—quickly caught on. Four major revivals of *Porgy and Bess* have been mounted on Broadway since the first engagement. In 1942, again with Todd Duncan and Anne Brown, it ran 286 performances in a somewhat trimmed down version. In 1952, as part of a four-year international tour, it returned with William Warfield and Leontyne Price and ran for 305 performances. An acclaimed production in 1976 by the Houston Grand Opera Company featured Donnie Ray Albert as Porgy and Clamma Dale as Bess, and had a 122-performance run on Broadway. A 1983 production was based on the 1976 version and was the first dramatic work ever staged at the Radio City Music hall. It gave 45 performances. The Metropolitan Opera produced the work in 1985, the first performaces ever given in that house.

SHENANDOAH

MUSIC: Gary Geld
LYRICS: Peter Udell
BOOK: James Lee Barrett, Peter Udell and Philip Rose (Based on a screenplay by James Lee Barrett)
DIRECTOR: Philip Rose
CHOREOGRAPHER: Robert Tucker
OPENED: 1/7/75, New York

Shenandoah is a traditional musical concerned with a strong-willed Virginia widower and his determination to prevent his family from becoming involved in the Civil War. John Cullums' robust performance and the play's old-fashioned morality found favor with Broadway audiences for well over two years. The three selections in this volume are representative of the scope of the prinicipal role of Charlie, and enormous baritone role that lies in the territory between musical theatre and full-fledged opera.

SHOW BOAT

MUSIC: Jerome Kern
LYRICS AND BOOK: Oscar Hammerstein II
DIRECTOR: Zeke Colvan
CHOREOGRAPHER: Sammy Lee
OPENED: 12/27/27, New York

No show ever to hit Broadway was more historically important, and at the same time more beloved, than *Show Boat*, that landmark of the 1927 season. Edna Ferber's novel of life on the Mississippi was the source for this musical/operetta, and provided a rich plot and characters which Kern and Hammerstein amplified to become some of the most memorable ever to grace the stage. *Show Boat* is not only a summing up of all that had come before it, both in the musical and operetta genres, but plants a seed of complete congruity which later further blossoms in the more adventurous shows of the '30s, '40s, and '50s. Almost every song in the show is a familiar gem: "Make Believe"; "Can't Help Lovin' Dat Man"; "You Are Love"; "Why Do I Love You?"; "Bill"; and that most classic song of the musical stage, "Ol' Man River." A Hal Prince production of the show opened on Broadway in 1994, and later toured nationally.

SOUTH PACIFIC

MUSIC: Richard Rodgers
LYRICS: Oscar Hammerstein II
BOOK: Oscar Hammerstein II and Joshua Logan
DIRECTOR: Joshua Logan
OPENED: 4/7/49, New York

South Pacific had the second longest Broadway run of the nine musicals with songs by Richard Rodgers and Oscar Hammerstein II. Director Joshua Logan first urged the partners to adapt a short story, "Fo' Dolla," contained in James Michener's book about World War II, *Tales of the South Pacific*. Rodgers and Hammerstein, however, felt that the story—about Lt. Joe Cable's tender romance with Liat, a Polynesian girl—was a bit too much like Madame Butterfly, and they suggested that another story in the collection, "Our Heroine," should provide the main plot. This one was about the unlikely attraction between Nellie Forbush, a naïve Navy nurse from Little Rock, and Emile de Becque, a sophisticated French planter living on a Pacific island. The tales were combined by having Cable and de Becque go on a dangerous mission together behind Japanese lines. Coming just a few years after the war, and featuring several veterans in the cast, the show was enormously resonant with 1949 audiences. But there has not so far been a major Broadway revival. Perhaps because of its daring (for the time) theme of the evils of racial prejudice, it was also the second musical to be awarded the prestigious Pulitzer Prize for Drama. This production was the first of two musicals (the other was *The Sound of Music*) in which Mary Martin, who played Nellie, was seen as a Rodgers and Hammerstein heroine. It also marked the Broadway debut of famed Metropolitan Opera basso, Ezio Pinza, who played de Becque. Mitzi Gaynor and Rossano Brazzi starred in 20th Century-Fox's 1958 film version, also directed by Logan.

THE THREEPENNY OPERA

MUSIC: Kurt Weill
WORDS: Bertolt Brecht
ENGLISH TRANSLATION: Marc Blitzstein
OPENED: 1928 (Berlin), 3/10/54 (New York)

The premiere of *The Threepenny Opera* in 1928 marked the 200th anniversary of *The Beggar's Opera*, and the earlier work is the basis for the famous Brecht-Weill collaboration. It revealed a revolutionary new style of German musical theatre, full of sardonic wit and political power. "Mack the Knife" has proven to be a durably popular product of the show, recorded and performed in widely varying styles and arrangements. Although the show had been performed in New York as early as the '30s, it didn't gain wide popularity until the famous 1954 production which starred Weill's widow, Lotte Lenya. That production went on to boast one of the longest runs in New York theatrical history, and the show continues to frequently appear on stages around the world.

EVERYBODY SAYS DON'T
from *Anyone Can Whistle*

Words and Music by STEPHEN SONDHEIM

Allegro moderato

HAPGOOD:

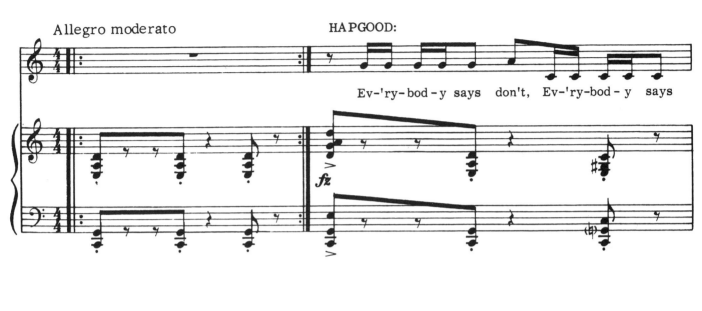

Ev-'ry-bod-y says don't, Ev-'ry-bod-y says

don't, Ev-'ry-bod-y says don't, it is-n't right. Don't! It is-n't nice!

Ev-'ry-bod-y says don't, Ev-'ry-bod-y says don't, Ev-'ry-bod-y says: don't walk on the

grass, Don't dis-turb the peace, Don't skate on the ice.

Well, I say do!

I say Walk on the grass, it was meant to feel! I Say

Sail! Tilt at the wind-mill And if you fail, you fail!

Ev-'ry-bod-y says don't, Ev-'ry-bod-y says don't, Ev-'ry-bod-y says: don't get out of

line. When they say that, then, La-dy, that's a sign: _____ Nine times out of

ten, La-dy, you are do-ing just fine! _____

Make just a rip-ple. _____ Come on, be brave. _____

This time a rip-ple, ——— Next time a wave! ———

Some-times you have to start small, Climb-ing the ti-ni-est wall,

May-be you're go-ing to fall, —— But it's bet-ter than not start-ing at all!

Ev-'ry-bod-y says no, Ev-'ry-bod-y says stop, Ev-'ry-bod-y says: must-n't rock the

boat! Must-n't touch a thing! _____ Ev-'ry-bod-y says

don't, Ev-'ry-bod-y says wait, Ev-'ry-bod-y says: can't fight Cit-y Hall. Can't

— up-set the cart, Can't__ laugh at the King. _____

— Well, I say try! _____

I say: Laugh at the kings or they'll make you cry!

Lose your poise! _____ Fall if you have to,

But, la-dy, make a noise! _ *(Spoken)* Ev-'ry-bod-y says

(Sung) don't, Ev-'ry-bod-y says can't, Ev-'ry-bod-y says: wait a-round for mir-a-cles,___

That's the way the world is made! _____ I in - sist on

Mir - a - cles, ___ if you do them, Mir - a - cles! __

Noth - ing to them! I say don't-- Don't be a -

fraid! _____

C'EST MOI
from *Camelot*

Words by ALAN JAY LERNER
Music by FREDERICK LOEWE

And here am I to give my all.   I

know in my soul what you ex-pect of me; And all that and

more I shall be! _____ A   knight of the ta - ble round should be in-re-
soul of a knight should be a thing re -

$(\bd = \bd)$ Alla marcia

vin - ci -ble;   Suc - ceed where a less fan - tas - tic man would fail; _____
mark - a -ble: His heart and his mind as pure as morn - ing dew. _____

man so extra - or - di - naire? _____ C'est
man so un - touch'd and pure? _____ *(Spoken modestly) C'est moi...C'est

en dehors

Allegretto scherzando

moi! C'est moi, I'm forced to ad - mit! 'Tis I, I hum - bly re - ply. _____ That
moi! C'est moi, I blush to dis - close, I'm far too no - ble to lie. _____ That

p

mor - tal who These mar - vels can do, C'est moi, C'est moi, 'tis I! _____ I've
man in whom These qual - i - ties bloom, C'est moi, C'est moi, 'tis I! _____ I've

mp

nev - er lost in bat - tle or game. I'm sim - ply the best by
nev - er stray'd From all I be - lieve. I'm bless'd with an i - ron

*2nd stanza only

CAMELOT
from *Camelot*

Words by ALAN JAY LERNER
Music by FREDERICK LOEWE

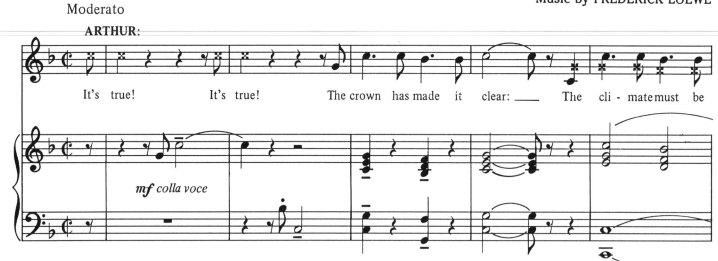

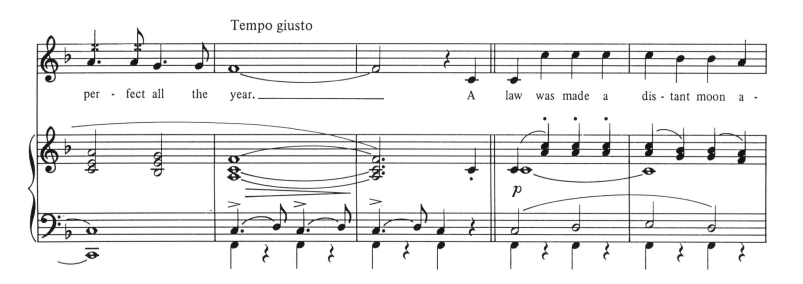

And there's a le-gal lim-it to the snow here _____ In
Ca - me - lot. The win - ter is for -
bid - den till De - cem - ber _____ And ex - its March the sec - ond on the
dot. By or - der sum - mer ling - ers through Sep - tem - ber _____

The rain may nev-er fall till aft-er sun-down. _____ By

eight the morn-ing fog must dis-ap - pear. _____ In short, there's sim-ply

poco rit.

not A more con-gen-ial spot For happ'-ly-ev-er - aft-er-ing than

poco rit.

Poco meno mosso   *accel.*   Tempo giusto

here In Ca - me - lot.

f *leggiero sempre*

accel.

Ca-me-lot!   Ca-me-lot!   I know it

gives a per-son pause,   But in Ca-me-lot,

Ca-me-lot,   Those are the le-gal laws.

HOW TO HANDLE A WOMAN
from *Camelot*

Words by ALAN JAY LERNER
Music by FREDERICK LOEWE

And what of teach-ing me by turn-ing me to an-i-mal and bird, From beav-er to the small-est bob-o-link! I should have had a whirl At chang-ing to a girl, To

learn the way the crea - tures think!

But

Tranquillo

was-n't there a night, on a sum-mer long gone by, We pass'd a cou-ple wran-gling a - way;___ And

did I not say, Mer - lyn: What if that chap were I? And did he not give coun-sel and say...___ What

was it now? My mind's a wall._____ Oh, yes! By jove, now I re - call:_____

Moderato

How to han-dle a wom-an? There's a way, said the wise old man; A

way known by ev - 'ry wom-an Since the whole rig-'ma-role be - gan. Do I

flat-ter her? I begged him an - swer. Do I threat-en or ca-jole or plead? Do I

brood or play the gay ro-manc-er? Said he, smil-ing: No in-deed. How to han-dle a wom-an? Mark me well, I will tell you, Sir: The way to han-dle a wom-an Is to love her... simp-ly love her... Mere-ly love her...

IF EVER I WOULD LEAVE YOU

from *Camelot*

Words by ALAN JAY LERNER
Music by FREDERICK LOEWE

Moderato

LANCELOT: *(Sings a madrigal to GUENEVERE.)*

This, I know, will e'er be so: The rea-son to live is on-ly to love A

god-dess on earth and a God a-bove.

Con espressione

If ev-er I would leave you ____ It would-n't be in

sum - mer; _____ See - ing you in sum - mer, I nev - er would

go. _____ Your hair streaked with sun - light... _____ Your lips red as

flame... _____ Your face with a lus - tre _____ That puts gold to

shame. _____ But if I'd ev - er leave you, _____ it could - n't be in

au - tumn. _____ How I'd leave in au - tumn, I nev - er would

know. _____ I've seen how you spar - kle _____ When fall nips the

air. _____ I know you in au - tumn _____ And I must be

there. And could I leave you run - ning mer - ri - ly through the

snow? _____ Or on a win-try eve-ning when you catch the fi-re's

glow? _____ If ev-er I would leave you, _____ How could it be in

spring - time, _____ Know-ing how in spring I'm be - witch'd by you

so? _____ Oh, no, not in spring - time! _____ Sum-mer, win-ter or

fall! _____ No, nev-er could I leave you _____ at

all. _____

stringendo e cresc. *passionato*

If ev-er I would leave you, _____ How could it be in

spring - time, _____ Know - ing how in spring I'm be - witch'd by you

so? _____ Oh, no, not in spring - time! _____ Sum - mer, win - ter or

fall! _____ No, nev - er could I leave you _____ at

all. _____

RIVER IN THE RAIN
from *Big River*

Music and Lyrics by
ROGER MILLER

IF I LOVED YOU
from *Carousel*

Words by OSCAR HAMMERSTEIN II
Music by RICHARD RODGERS

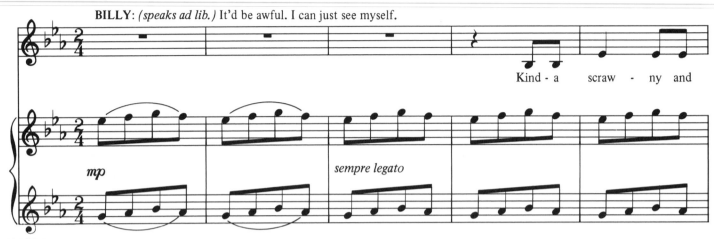

All I'd want you to know._____

If I loved you, Words would-n't come__ in an eas - y way

'Round in cir - cles I'd go!_____

Long - in' to tell you, but a - fraid and shy.

SOLILOQUY
from *Carousel*

Words by OSCAR HAMMERSTEIN II
Music by RICHARD RODGERS

won-der what he'll think of me!___ I guess he'll call me "The old man!"___ I guess he'll think I can lick Ev-'ry oth-er fel-ler's fa-ther; Well, I can!___ I bet that he'll turn out to be___ The spit-an' im-age Of his Dad.___ But he'll have

more com-mon sence Than his pud-din' head-ed fa-ther ev-er had._____ I'll

Più mosso

teach him to wras-sle, And dive through a wave, When we go in the morn-in's for our

swim. His moth-er can teach him The way to be-have, But she

won't make a sis-sy out o' him. Not him! Not my boy! Not

62

fun with a son, But you got to be a fa-ther To a girl! _____

_____ She might-n't be so bad at that, _____ A kid with

rib-bons In her hair! _____ A kind o' neat and pe-tite Lit-tle

tin-type of her moth-er! What a pair! _____

(Spoken) I can just hear myself
bragging about her!

She has a few Pink and white young fel-lers of two and three But my lit-tle girl Gets hun-gry ev-'ry night and she comes home to

Poco più mosso

(Spoken) My little girl, my little girl!

me! I got to get read-y be-fore she comes! I got to make cer-tain that she Won't be dragged up in slums With a

TEN MINUTES AGO
from *Cinderella*

Lyrics by OSCAR HAMMERSTEIN II
Music by RICHARD RODGERS

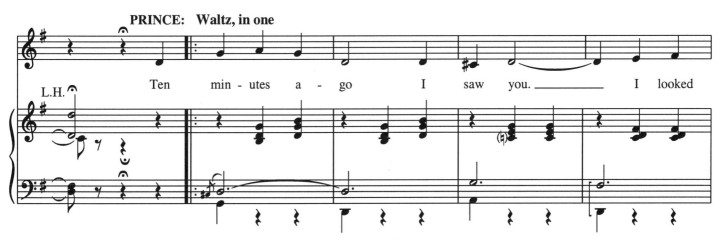

The song is sung twice in the show, first by the Prince, then by Cinderella.

up when you came through the door. _____ My head start-ed

reel - ing, You gave me the feel - ing the room had no

ceil - ing or floor. _____ Ten min - utes a - go I

met you _____ And we mur-mured our how-do-you-do's. _____

fly - ing _____ And she's tak - ing me back to the

skies. _____ In the arms of my love I'm fly - ing _____

_____ O - ver moun - tain and mead - ow and glen, _____

_____ And I like it so well that for all I can tell I may

never come down a - gain! _____ I may

nev - er come down to earth a -

1
gain. _____ Ten

2
gain! _____

8va

DO I LOVE YOU BECAUSE YOU'RE BEAUTIFUL?

from *Cinderella*

Words by OSCAR HAMMERSTEIN II
Music by RICHARD RODGERS

PRINCE:
Do I love you be-cause you're beau-ti-ful? Or are you beau-ti-ful be-cause I love you? Am I mak-ing be-lieve I see in you a girl too

love - ly to_____ be real - ly true? Do I want you be-cause you're won - der-ful?_____ Or are you won - der-ful _____ be-cause I want you? _____ Are you the sweet in - ven-tion of a lov - er's dream, ___ Or are you real - ly as beau - ti - ful as you seem. _____

Largo

MARRY ME A LITTLE

from *Company*

Music and Lyrics by
STEPHEN SONDHEIM

Allegro appassionata (♩ = 80)

Mar-ry me _____ a lit-tle, Love me just _____ e-nough.

Cry, _ but _____ not too of-ten, Play, _ but _____ not too rough.

Keep a ten - der dis - tance, So we'll both _____ be free.

Not ex - clu - sive-ly.   That's the way _____ it ought to

be. _____ I'm read - y!

I'm read - y now! _____

Just _ the ____ sim - ple stuff. Keep a ten - der dis - tance

So we'll both ___ be free. That's the way ___ it ought to

be. _____ I'm read - y!

Mar-ry me ___ a lit-tle, Bod-y, heart ___ and soul.

Pas-sion - ate _____ as hell, But Al-ways in _____ con-trol.

Want me first _____ and fore - most, Keep me com - pan-y.

That's the way _____ it ought to be. _____

I'm read - y! I'm read - y!

now! _____

mf legato　　　*dim.*

p

Oh, how gent - ly we'll talk, _____

Oh, how soft - ly we'll tread. _____

All the stings, ___ The ug - ly things __

We'll keep _____ un - said. _____

We'll build a _____ co -

coon Of love and _____

re - spect. You

prom - ise _____ what - ev - er you

like, I'll nev - er col - lect. _____

_____ Right?

O - kay, then, I'm read - y!

SORRY-GRATEFUL
from *Company*

Words and Music by STEPHEN SONDHEIM

In the show Harry, Larry and David alternate verses in this song.

still you doubt,___ And she goes out.___ Ev-'ry-thing's diff-'rent,

Noth-ing's changed,___ On - ly may - be slight - ly re - ar - ranged.___ You're

poco rall.

sor - ry — grate - ful, Re - gret-ful — hap - py; Why look for an - swers where

pp a tempo

none oc - cur?___ You al - ways are___ what you al - ways were,___ Which has

pp

Strict rhythm

noth-ing to do with, All to do with her. You're

al-ways sor-ry,__ You're al-ways grate-ful,__ You hold her, think-ing,__ "I'm

not a lone." You're still a lone.__ You

don't live for__ her, You do live with__ her. You're scared she's start-ing to

drift a-way,___ And scared she'll stay.___ Good things get bet-ter,

Bad get worse.___ Wait, I think I meant that in re-verse.___ You're

Tempo I°

sor-ry — grate-ful, Re - gret-ful — hap-py. Why look for an-swers where

none oc - cur?___ You'll al-ways be___ what you al-ways were,___ Which has

noth-ing to do with, All to do with her._____ You'll

al-ways be__ what you al-ways were,__ Which has noth-ing to do with, All to do with

Strict rhythm

her._____ Noth-ing to do with, All to do with

her._____

ppp

WHEN I WAS A LAD
from *HMS Pinafore*

Words by W. S. GILBERT
Music by ARTHUR SULLIVAN

Allegro non troppo

SIR JOSEPH PORTER:

When I was a lad I served a term As
As of-fice boy I made such a mark That they

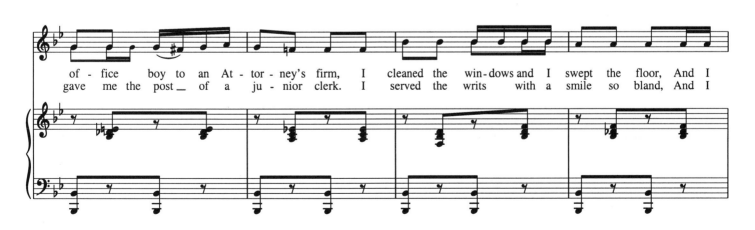

of - fice boy to an At - tor - ney's firm, I cleaned the win-dows and I swept the floor, And I
gave me the post __ of a ju - nior clerk. I served the writs with a smile so bland, And I

po - lished up the han - dle of the big front door.
co - pied all the let - ters in a big round hand.

I po - lished up that han - dle so care - ful - lee, That
I co - pied all the let - ters in a hand so free, That

now I am the ru - ler of the Queen's Na - vee!
now I am the ru - ler of the Queen's Na - vee!

I grew so rich that I was sent By a
Now lands-men all, who - ev - er you may be, If you

pock - et bor - ough in - to Par - lia - ment. I al - wys vo - ted at my
want to rise ___ to the top of the tree, If your soul is - n't fet - tered to an

par - ty's call, And I nev - er thought of think-ing for my - self at all.
of - fice stool, Be care - ful to be guid - ed by this gold - en rule,

I thought so lit - tle, they re - ward - ed me, By
Stick close to your desks and nev - er go to sea, And you

mak - ing me the ru - ler of the Queen's Na - vee.
all may be ru - lers of the Queen's Na - vee.

TRY TO REMEMBER
from *The Fantasticks*

Words by TOM JONES
Music by HARVEY SCHMIDT

life was so ten-der That no one wept ex-cept the

wil-low. Try to re-mem-ber when life was so ten-der That

dreams were kept be-side your pil-low. Try to re-

mem-ber when life was so ten-der That love was an em-ber a-

bout to bil - low. Try to re - mem - ber and if you re -

poco rall.

mp a tempo

mem - ber, Then fol - low.___

pp

Fol - low___

p

Fol - low___

mp

cem - ber, it's nice to re - mem - ber The fire of Sep -

tem - ber that made us mel - low. Deep in De - cem - ber our

poco rall. *p a tempo*

hearts should re - mem - ber, And fol - low.

rit. *a tempo*

pp , *p*

pochissimo accel. *rall. al fine* *p*

8va

THE ROAD YOU DIDN'T TAKE

from *Follies*

Words and Music by STEPHEN SONDHEIM

There is - n't time for an - y more.

One's life con - sists of ei - ther / or. One has re -

grets which one for - gets, And as the

years go on, The

road you did-n't take hard-ly comes to mind, Does it?_____ The

door you did-n't try, Where could it have led?_____ The

choice you did-n't make nev-er was de-fined, Was it?_____

Dreams you did-n't dare_____ are dead. Were they ev-er there?_____ Who said? I

don't re - mem - ber, I don't re - mem - ber at

all. _____

books I'll nev - er read would - n't change a thing, Would they? _____ The

girls I'll nev-er know, I'm too ti-red for._____ The

lives I'll nev-er lead could-n't make me sing, Could they?____

Could they?____ Could they?____ Chanc-es that you miss,_____ Ig-nore.

Ig-nor-ance is bliss;_____ What's more, you won't re-mem-ber, You

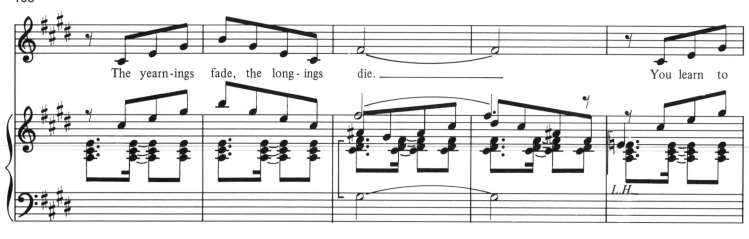

The yearn-ings fade, the long-ings die._____ You learn to

bid them all good - bye._____ And oh, the peace,_____ the bless - ed

peace._____ At last you come to know;_____

The roads you nev - er take go through rock - y

WHEN YOU'RE LYING AWAKE

from *Iolanthe*

Words by W.S. GILBERT
Music by ARTHUR SULLIVAN

some-thing be-tween a large bath-ing ma-chine and a ver-y small sec-ond-class car-riage — And you're

giv-ing a treat (pen-ny ice and cold meat) to a par-ty of friends and re-la-tions — They're a

rav-en-ous horde — and they all came on board at Sloane Square and South Ken-sing-ton Sta-tions. And

bound on that jour-ney you find your at-tor-ney (who start-ed that morn-ing from Dev-on); He's a

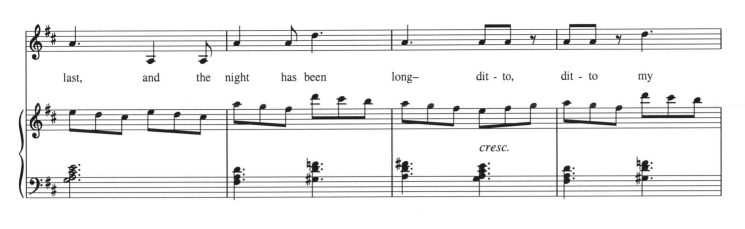

last, and the night has been long– dit - to, dit - to my

a piacere

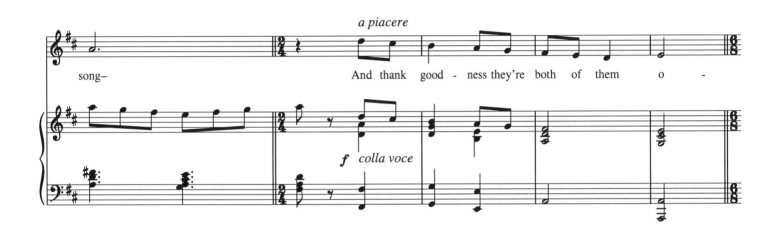

song– And thank good - ness they're both of them o -

(Lord Chancellor falls exhausted on a seat.)

ver!

Con fuoco

WERE THINE THAT SPECIAL FACE

from *Kiss Me, Kate*

Words and Music by COLE PORTER

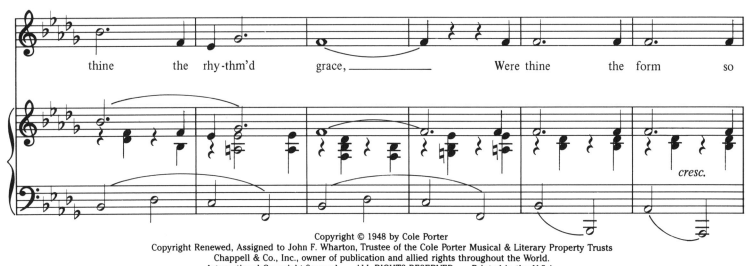

Then you'll be mine, all mine.

f *a tempo*

Quasi recitativo and tenderly

I wrote a po - em in clas - sic style I wrote it with my

p dolce

tongue in my cheek And my lips in a smile. But of late my po - em

pp

poco sostenuto

Has a mean - ing so new, For, to my sur - prise, It sud-den-ly ap-plies to my dar - ling, To

WHERE IS THE LIFE THAT LATE I LED?

from *Kiss Me, Kate*

Allegro con fuoco

Words and Music by COLE PORTER

PETRUCHIO: Since I reached _____ the charm - ing age of pu - ber - ty, _____ I be - gan _____ to fin - ger fem - i - nine curls. _____ Like a

show _____ that's typ - i - cal - ly Shu - bert - y, _____ I have

al - ways had a mult - i - tude of girls. _____ But

much broader-ad lib

now that a mar - ried man, _____ at last, am I, _____ How a-

Tempo I

ware of my dear, de - part - ed past am I. _____ Where is the

Refrain:

life that late I led? Where is it now? To-tal-ly dead. Where is the fun I used to find? Where has it gone? Gone with the wind. A

mar - ried life_____ may all be well_____ But

rais - ing an heir Could nev - er com - pare With rais - ing a bit of

hell. So I re - peat what first I_____ said,_____

Where is the life that late I, In dear Mi -

la - no, ____ where are you, Mo - mo, ____ Still sell - ing those pic - tures of the scrip - tures in the

Duo - mo? ____ And Ca - ro - li - na, ____ Where are you Li - na, ____ Still ped - dling your

piz - za in the streets o' Ta - or - mi - na? ____ And in Fi - ren - ze, ____ where are you,

A - lice, ____ Still there in your pret - ty, it - ty - bit - ty Pit - ti pal - ace? ____ And sweet Luc -

*Pronounced "Caroleena"   ** "Leena"

re - tia, _____ so young and gay - ee? _____ What scan-da-lous do - in's in the ru - ins of Pom -

pe - ii! _____ Where is the life that late I _____

led? _____ Where is it now? _____ To - tal - ly

dead. _____ Where is the fun I used to _____

find? _____ Where has it gone? _____ Gone with the

wind. _____ The mar - riage game _____ is

quite al - right. _____ Yes, dur - ing the day it's eas - y to play, But

oh, what a bore at night. So I re - peat what first I _____

*Pronounced "Leeza"

To - tal - ly dead. Where is the fun I used to find? Where has it gone? Gone with the wind. I've oft' been told of nup - tial bliss, But what do you do, at quar - ter to two, With

ad lib.

ff fz p p

on-ly a shrew to kiss? So I re-peat what first I ____ said: ____

____ Where is the life that late ____ I ____

led? ____

MARIAN THE LIBRARIAN
from Meredith Willson's *The Music Man*

By MEREDITH WILLSON

catch your ear? I love you mad - ly, mad - ly, Mad - am li -

brar - i - an, Mar - i - an. Heav-en help us, if the li - brar - y caught on

fi - re, and the vol - un - teer hose - bri - gade-men had to whis-per the news to

Mar - i - an,

Mad-am li - brar - i - an.

What can I say, my dear, to make it clear? I need you bad - ly, bad - ly, Mad-am li - brar - i - an, Mar - i - an. If I stum-bled, and I bust-ed my what-you-ma -

140

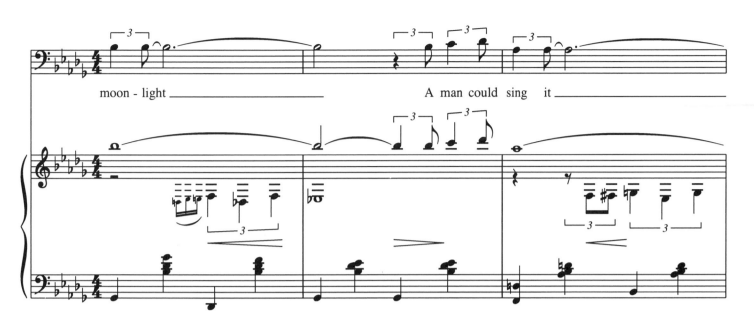

moon - light _____ A man could sing it _____

_____ in the moon - light. _____

And a fel-low would know that his dar-ling___ had heard ev-'ry word of his song with the

moon-light _____ help-ing a - long. _____

But when I try, in here, to tell you, dear, I

love you mad-ly, mad-ly, Mad-am li-brar-i-an, Mar-i-an, it's a long lost cause I can

nev-er win, for the civ-il-ized world ac - cepts as un-for-giv-a-ble sin an-y talk-ing out

SEPTEMBER SONG
from *Knickerbocker Holiday*

Words by MAXWELL ANDERSON
Music by KURT WEILL

Moderato assai

STUYVESANT:

When I was a young man court - ing the girls I

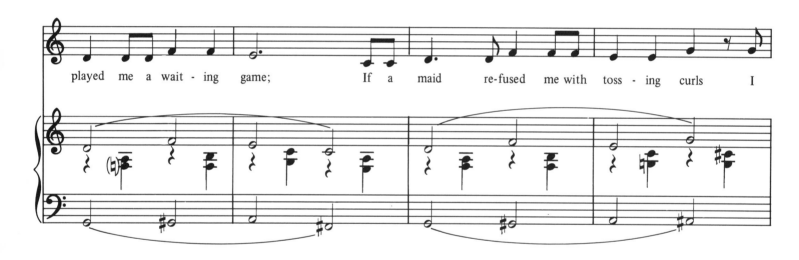

played me a wait - ing game; If a maid re-fused me with toss - ing curls I

let the old earth take a cou-ple of whirls While I plied her with tears in place of pearls And as

time came a-round she came my way, As time came a-round she came.

But it's a long, long while From May to De-cem-ber—

And the days grow short——————— When you reach Sep-tem-ber,—

And I have lost one tooth and I walk a lit-tle lame,

And I have-n't got time_____ for the wait - ing game,

For the days turn to gold_____ as they grow few,_____

Sep - tem - ber, No - vem - ber,_____

And these few gold - en days I'd spend with you,

These gold-en days I'd spend with you.

When you meet with the young men earl-y in spring They court you in song and rhyme, They woo you with words and a clo-ver ring But if you ex-am-ine the goods they bring They have lit-tle to of-fer but the songs they sing And a plen-ti-ful waste of

time of day, A plen-ti-ful waste of time. And it's a long, long while

from May to De-cem-ber___ Will a clo-ver ring last___

___till you reach Sep-tem-ber?___ I'm not quite e-quipped

for the wait-ing game, But I have a lit-tle mon-ey___

LOST IN THE STARS

from *Lost in the Stars*

Words by MAXWELL ANDERSON
Music by KURT WEILL

STEPHEN:

Be-fore Lord God made the sea and the land, He held all the stars in the palm of his hand, And they ran through his fin-gers like grains of ___ sand, And one lit-tle star fell a-lone. Then the

Lord God hunt-ed through the wide night air For the lit-tle dark star on the

wind down_ there. And he stat - ed and prom-ised he'd take spec-ial care So it

mf Poco più mosso

would-n't get lost a - gain. Now a man don't mind if the

stars grow dim And the clouds blow o - ver and dark - en him, So

long as the Lord God's watch-ing o-ver them, Keep-ing track how it all goes on. But I've been walk-ing through the night and the day Till my eyes get wear-y and my head turns gray, And some-times it seems may-be God's gone a-way, For-get-ting the prom-ise that we heard him say,

rall. Tempo I°

cresc.

THOUSANDS OF MILES
from *Lost in the Stars*

Words by MAXWELL ANDERSON
Music by KURT WEILL

miles._____ The lines on the map stretch

far and thin, To the streets and days that close him

in, But then as of old _____ he turns 'round to grin _____

_____ o - ver thou - sands, thou - sands of miles. Not

THIS IS THE LIFE

from *Love Life*

Words by ALAN JAY LERNER
Music by KURT WEILL

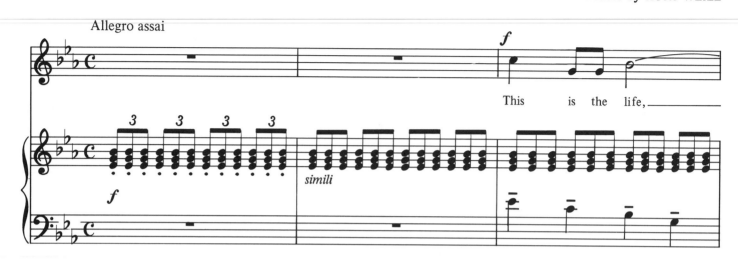

I'm free!

I can be as slop-py as I damn well please, I can sprawl on the bed at my lei-sure and ease, I can throw my ash-es all a-round the floor, I can read all night, I can

e - ven snore. The clos - et's mine, ev -'ry hang - er in there. No more

load - ed hooks do I ev - er share. The tub is mine! The

sink is mine! The chair is mine! The room is mine!

Yes, sir - ee!_____ This is the life._____

The life for me! _____ I'm

free. _____

ff

molto rit.

Andante cantabile

p

Sure, I miss the kids I guess, I miss them more than I could ev - er

p

say. But I am told that time will make it less and I'll grow

ought to be! _____ I'm free! *(Speaks into telephone)*

Room service! It's great when you're hun - gry to phone be - low And

not have to wait till your wife... Hel - lo!

My name is Sam - u'l Coo - per in sev - en - twen - ty - eight. I like to or - der din - ner be -

fore it is too late. I'll have shrimps and steak, make it

me - dium well, and the rich-est des-sert __ in the whole ho - tel, But

speed is im - por-tant. Bring it on the run. I'm hun-gry!... *(Spoken)* What?

f Yes, I said for one! You heard me! Damn it! Ser - vice for one!

Molto meno mosso

Why do they ask me ev - 'ry time I phone?

What's so biz - zare a - bout a man a - lone?

Andante cantabile

Sure I know it's not i - deal I still have

thoughts of her I can't for - get. But that's a thing they say that time will heal. I won - der

Allargando

dope! You're ab-so-lute-ly free!

I

Moderato assai

wish I were free of that dream I keep dream-ing. The three of them swim-ming, then

start-ing to drown. And I'm some-where else and I don't hear them scream-ing...

And thou-sands of peo-ple just watch them go down.

DULCINEA
from *Man of La Mancha*

Words by JOE DARION
Music by MITCH LEIGH

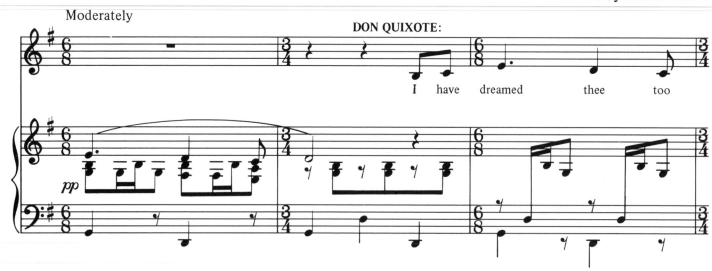

DON QUIXOTE:

I have dreamed thee too

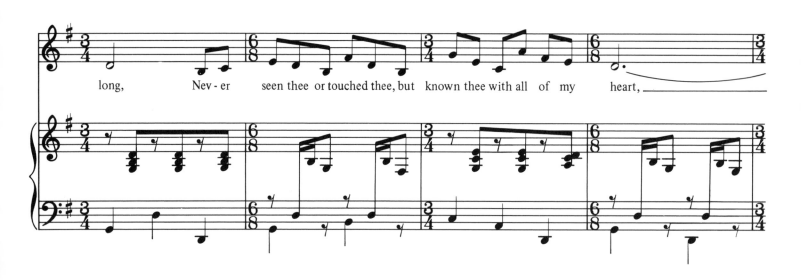

long, Nev-er seen thee or touched thee, but known thee with all of my heart,

Half a prayer, half a song, Thou hast al-ways been with me, though

we have been al-ways a - part. _____ Dul - ci - ne - a... _____

_____ Dul - ci - ne - a... _____ I see heav - en when I

see thee, Dul - ci - ne - a, _____ And thy name is like a

prayer an an - gel whis - pers... _____ Dul - ci - ne - a... _____

Dul-ci-ne-a! If I reach out to thee, Do not trem-ble and shrink from the touch of my hand on thy hair, Let my fin - gers but see Thou art warm and a - live, and no phan-tom to fade in the air. Dul-ci - ne-a...

Dul-ci-ne-a... I have sought thee, sung thee,

dreamed thee, Dul-ci-ne-a! Now I've found thee, and the

world shall know thy glo - ry, Dul-ci-ne-a...

rall.

A tempo

Dul-ci-ne-a!

THE IMPOSSIBLE DREAM
(THE QUEST)
from *Man of La Mancha*

Words by JOE DARION
Music by MITCH LEIGH

180

MAN OF LA MANCHA
(I, DON QUIXOTE)
from *Man of La Mancha*

Words by JOE DARION
Music by MITCH LEIGH

Tempo Paso Doble

DON QUIXOTE:

Hear me now, oh __ thou bleak and un - bear - a - ble world, Thou art base and __ de - bauched as can be; __ And a knight with __ his ban - ners all brave - ly __ un -

In the show this is sung as a duet between Don Quixote and Sancho Panza.

furled Now hurls down his gaunt-let to thee! _____

____ I am I, Don Qui-xo-te, The Lord of __ La

Man-cha, My des-tin-y calls and I go, _____

_____ And the wild winds of for-tune will car-ry me

ser - pents of sin! All your das - tard - ly do - ings are

past, _____ For a ho - ly __ en - deav - or is

now to __ be - gin And vir - tue __ shall

tri - umph at last! _____

LONELY ROOM
from *Oklahoma!*

Words by OSCAR HAMMERSTEIN II
Music by RICHARD RODGERS

189

out like I want them to be And I'm bet-ter 'n that smart Al - eck cow - hand Who thinks he is bet - ter 'n me! And the girl that I want ain't a-fraid of my arms, And her

own soft arms keep me warm. And her

long, yel-ler hair falls a-crost my face, Jist like the rain in a storm!

Moderato

The floor creaks, The door squeaks, And the

mouse starts a - nib-blin' on the broom. And the sun flicks my eyes, It was

OH, WHAT A BEAUTIFUL MORNIN'
from *Oklahoma!*

Words by OSCAR HAMMERSTEIN II
Music by RICHARD RODGERS

bright, gold-en haze on the mead-ow, ___ There's a bright, gold-en

194

haze on the mead-ow,___ The corn is as high as an el - e - phant's

eye, An' it looks like it's climb-in' clear up to the sky.

pp *a tempo* *poco rit*

Moderato

Oh, what a beau-ti-ful morn - in' Oh, what a

p *a tempo*

beau-ti-ful day___ I got a beau-ti-ful feel -

I got a beau-ti-ful feel-in',

Ev-'ry thin's go-in' my way.

All the sounds of the earth are like mu-sic,_____ All the

Oh, what a beau - ti - ful day, _____

I got a beau - ti - ful feel - in',

Ev - 'ry -thin's go - in' my way, _____

rit al fine

Oh, what a beau - ti - ful day. _____

sempre rit

pp

Ped. *

REVIEWING THE SITUATION

from the Columbia Pictures-Romulus Film *Oliver!*

Words and Music by
LIONEL BART

I'd be the first one to say that I was-n't a saint— I'm

find-ing it hard to be real-ly as black as they paint. ___ I'm re-view-ing ___

(♩ = 108)

___ the sit-u-a-tion. ___ Can a fel-low be a

vil-lain all his life? ___ All the tri-als ___

how to win friends and to in-flu-ence peo-ple, so how?__ I'm re - view-ing _____ the sit-u-

a - tion. _____ I must quick-ly look up ev-'ry-one I know: _____

__ Ti-tled peo-ple _____ with a sta-tion _____ Who can

help me make a real im-pres-sive show. _____ I will own a suite at

accel. poco a poco

accel. poco a poco

dear-est com-pan-ions have al-ways been vil-lains and thieves— So at

my time of life I should start turn-ing o-ver new leaves ___ I'm re-view-ing ___

(♩ = 108)

___ the sit-u-a-tion. _____ If you want to eat you've

got to earn a bob! _____ Is it such a _____

a piacere

think it out a - gain _____ What hap - pens when I'm

colla voce

sev - en - ty? Must come a time— Sev - en - ty When you're

old and it's cold and who cares if you live or you die. Your

($\dot{}$ = 108)

one con - so - la - tion's the mon - ey you may have put by _____ I'm re - view - ing _____

I GOT PLENTY O' NUTTIN'

from *Porgy and Bess*

Words by IRA GERSHWIN
and DUBOSE HEYWARD
Music by GEORGE GERSHWIN

In the context of the opera this includes chorus.

door,_____ 'Fraid some-bod-y's a - go-in' to rob 'em while dey's out a mak-in' more._____

_____ What for?_____ I got no lock on de door, (dat's no way to

be)._____ Dey kin steal de rug from de floor,_____ Dat's o-keh wid me, 'Cause de things dat I

prize, Like de stars in de skies, all are free._____ Oh, I got plen-ty o' nut-tin',_____ An'

me. I got de sun, got de moon, got de deep blue sea.

De folks wid plen-ty o' plen-ty Got to pray all de day.

Seems wid plen-ty you sure got to wor-ry how to keep de deb-ble a - way, a - way.

mf

I ain't a-fret-tin' 'bout hell Till de time ar - rive. Nev-er wor-ry long as I'm well,

Nev-er one to strive to be good, to be bad, what de hell, I is glad I's a-live. _____ Oh, I got plen-ty o'

nut-tin', _____ An' nut-tin's plen-ty fo' me. I got my gal, got my song, Got Heb-ben de whole day

long. No use com-plain-in', Got my gal, _____ got my Lawd, _____

(optional)

_____ got my song! _____

THEY CALL THE WIND MARIA
from *Paint Your Wagon*

Words by ALAN JAY LERNER
Music by FREDERICK LOEWE

Allegro Moderato

STEVE:

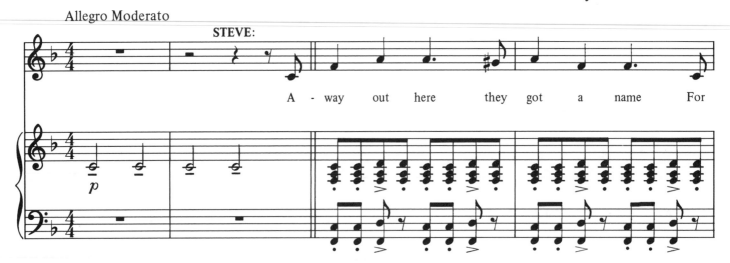

A - way out here they got a name For

wind and rain and fi - re; The rain is Tess, the

fi - re's Jo, And they call the wind Ma - ri - a.

ri - a! _____ They call the wind Ma -

Più vivo

ri - a! _____ Be - fore I knew Ma -

ri - a's name And heard her wail and whin - in', I

(simile)

had a girl and she had me, And the sun was al - ways

ain't no word but lone - ly. _____ And

I'm a lost and lone - ly man With - out a star to

guide me. Ma - ri - a, blow my love to me; I need my girl be -

Più mosso

side me. _____ Ma -

I AM THE VERY MODEL

from *The Pirates of Penzance*

Words by W.S. GILBERT
Music by ARTHUR SULLIVAN

square of the hy - pot - e - nuse.
fer - nal non-sense, *Pin - a - fore!*

I'm
Then

ver - y good at in - te - gral and dif - fer - en - tial cal - cu - lus; I know the sci - en - tif - ic names of
I can write a wash-ing bill in Bab - y - lon - ic cu - nei-form, And tell you ev - 'ry de - tail of Ca -

be - ings an - i - mal - cu - lous.
rac - ta - cus - 's u - ni - form: } In short, in mat - ters veg - e - ta - ble, an - i - mal, and min - er - al, I

am the ver - y mod - el of a mod - ern Ma - jor - Gen - er - al.

Slower

In fact, when I know what is meant by "mam-e-lon" and "rav-e-lin", When

I can tell at sight a Mau-ser ri-fle from a jav-e-lin, When such af-fairs as sor-ties and sur-

pris-es I'm more wa-ry at, And when I know pre-cise-ly what is meant by "com-mis-sa-ri-at", When

I have learnt what prog-ress has been made in mod-ern gun-ner-y, When I know more of tac-tics than a

nov-ice in a nun-ner-y— In short, when I've a smat-ter-ing of el-e-men-tal strat-e-gy—

(Bothered for a rhyme– struck with an idea)

You'll say a bet-ter Ma-jor-Gen-er-al has nev-er *sat* a gee—

For my mil-i-ta-ry know-ledge, tho' I'm

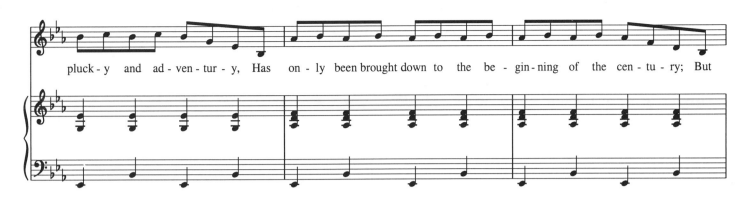

pluck - y and ad - ven - tur - y, Has on - ly been brought down to the be - gin - ning of the cen - tu - ry; But

still, in mat - ters veg - e - ta - ble, an - i - mal, and min - er - al, I am the ver - y mod - el of a

mod - ern Ma - jor - Gen - er - al.

I'VE HEARD IT ALL BEFORE

from *Shenandoah*

Music by GARY GELD
Words by PETER UDELL

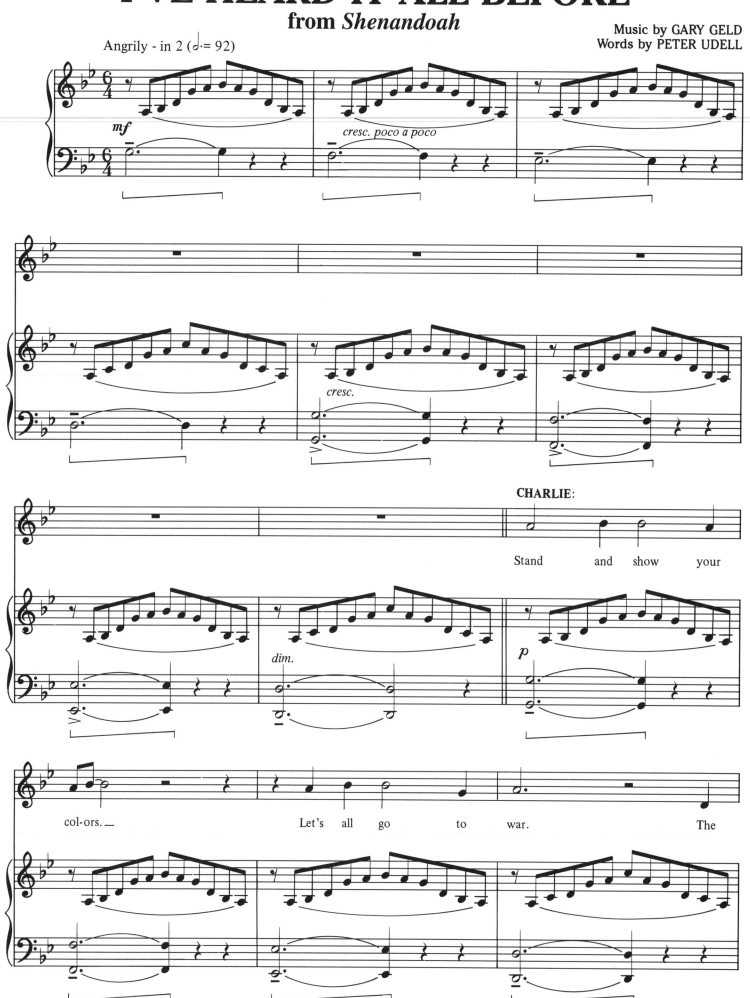

Tyr - an - y or jus - tice, an - ar - chy or law. We must de - fend our hon - or, I've heard it all be - fore. I've heard it all a hun-dred times I've heard it all be - fore. They

blame. _____ The trum-pet ____ sounds the

call to arms to leave the cit-ies

and the farms. ____ And al-ways the end-in' is the

same, the same, the same, the same. ____ The

MEDITATION I
from *Shenandoah*

Music by GARY GELD
Words by PETER UDELL

Hook up the mule and the plow. Got a Jen-ny and a Hen-ry An-der-son now; An ap - ple tree with a

Broader *(More deliberate)*   *a tempo*   *rall.*

fruit - ed bow; A lov - in' wife with child a - gain. And I'm think-in' I should sleep with the cow, Mar - tha,

p a tempo   *rall.*

Slowly   Moderato *(Slower than before)*

(Spoken:) Now, send for the Doc, no, I best go and bring 'im. Pour me a drink and I'll

yon-der in the barn with the cow. ____

p   *colla voce*   *lightly*

accel. to - - - - - - - - - -Tempo I   *rit.*   *molto rit.*

drink for joy.   *(Sings:)*

Get out the den-im, roll up the ging-ham, name him Ro - bert, he's a boy.

f rit.   *molto rit.*   *ff*

Meno mosso *(Sempre in 4)*

Ja - cob and James, _____ Na - than and John, _____ Jen - ny and

Slowly

(Spoken:) *(Sung:)*

Hen - ry and Ro - bert . . . and then You were gone, Mar-tha. _____

p > pp   *p*   *mf*

rall. *(Spoken:)* And . . . me . . . I got twenty-eight years in this farm, *(Sings:)*

My blood, my sweat and my

mp *rall.* *pp* *pp*

cresc. poco a poco - - - - - - - - - - - - -

tears in this farm, and no one's gon-na come a-long and say that I owe an - y part, not the

mp

cresc. poco a poco - - - - - - - -

MEDITATION II
from *Shenandoah*

Music by GARY GELD
Words by PETER UDELL

price of peace was more than I could

pay. I have no shame, I

lay the blame at some - one el - se's

door. And so the seeds of hate are sown that blow from war to

war._____ What for?_____ Oh, Lord,_____ what

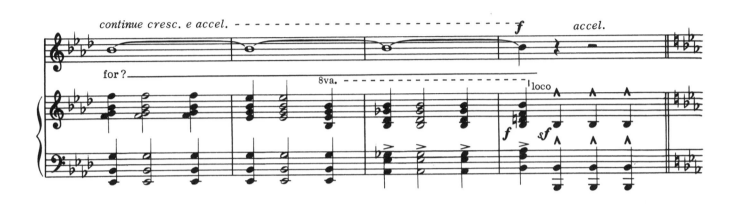

for?_____

North or South, they're all our__ chil-dren,

born of flesh in joy and in pain. They're yours and mine, our past and our fu-ture,

OL' MAN RIVER
from *Show Boat*

Words by OSCAR HAMMERSTEIN II
Music by JEROME KERN

*Joe is accompanied by chorus in this scene in the show.

Tote dat barge! Lift dat bale! Git a lit-tle drunk An' you land in jail.

colla voce

I git wear-y An' sick of try-in', I'm tired of liv-in' An' skeered of dy-in'; But

ol' man riv-er, He jes' keeps rol-lin' a - long!

Col-ored folks work on de Mis - sis - sip - pi, Col-ored folks work while de

white folks play. Pul - lin' dem boats from de dawn to sun - set,

Mosso

Git - tin' no rest till de Judg - ment Day. Don't look up an'

mf

don't look down, You don't dast make de white boss frown;

rall.

Bend yo' knees an' bow yo' head, an' pull dat rope un -

rall.

til yo're dead. Let me go 'way from de Mis - sis - sip - pi,

Let me go 'way from de white man boss. Show me dat stream called de

riv - er Jor - dan, Dat's de ol' stream dat I longs to cross!

Ol' man riv - er, Dat ol' man riv - er, He mus' know sump - in' But

SOME ENCHANTED EVENING

from *South Pacific*

Words by OSCAR HAMMERSTEIN II
Music by RICHARD RODGERS

then _____ That some-where you'll see her a - gain and a -

gain. _____ Some en - chant-ed eve - ning _____

Some one may be laugh - ing, _____ You may hear her laugh - ing _____ A - cross a

crowd - ed room And night af - ter night, _____ As strange as it

seems _____ The sound of her laugh-ter will sing in your

dreams. _____ Who can ex-plain it Who can tell you why?

Fools give you reas - ons, Wise men nev - er try. _____

Some en-chant-ed eve - ning _____ When you find your true love, _____

When you feel her call you___ A-cross a crowd-ed room, Then fly to her side___ And make her your own,___ Or all through your life you may dream all a-lone.___ Once you have found her, Nev-er let her go.

Once you have found her, Nev-er let her go!___

THIS NEARLY WAS MINE

from *South Pacific*

Words by OSCAR HAMMERSTEIN II
Music by RICHARD RODGERS

Tempo di Waltz espressivo

One dream in my heart_____ One

love to be liv - ing for _____ One love to be

liv - ing for _____ This near - ly was mine. _____

_____ One girl for my dream _____ One

part - ner in par - a - dise _____ This prom - ise of

par - a - dise_____ This near - ly was mine._____

Close to my heart she came_____ On - ly to fly a -

way_____ On - ly to fly as day flies from

moon - light._____ Now, now I'm a - lone_____

*Repeat can be started here.

Still dream-ing of par-a-dise, _____ Still

say-ing that par-a-dise _____ Once near-ly was mine. _____

Fine

So clear and deep are my fan - cies _____ Of things I

wish _____ were true _____ I'll keep re - mem - b'ring

MACK THE KNIFE
from *The Threepenny Opera*

English Words by MARC BLITZSTEIN
Original German Words by BERT BRECHT
Music by KURT WEILL

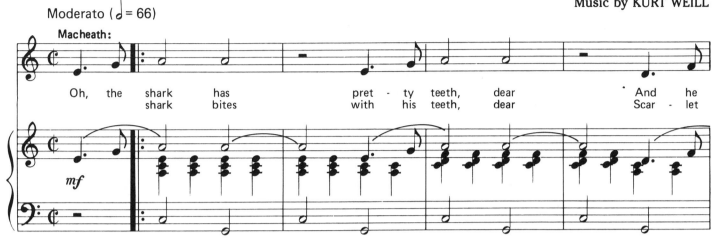

Knife? From a tug - boat by the

riv - er A ce - ment bag's drop - ping

down; The ce - ment's just for the

weight dear Bet you Mack - ie's back in town.